For $10,00
individual i

Do you like to squeeze other people's pimples and blackheads?

◆

Do you curl your toes or stretch them out during an orgasm?

◆

What part of the body turns you on the most?

◆

How sexually experienced do you want your marriage partner to be? How much is too much?

◆

If farting were considered a talent, how talented would you consider yourself?

◆

Does it bother you when people talk to you while you're on the toilet bowl?

Books by Maude Thickett

The Book of Outrageous Questions
Outrageously Offensive Jokes
Outrageously Offensive Jokes II
Outrageously Offensive Jokes III
Outrageously Offensive Jokes IV

Published by POCKET BOOKS

THE BOOK
OF
Outrageous
QUESTIONS

MAUDE THICKETT

POCKET BOOKS

New York   London   Toronto   Sydney   Tokyo

These questions may offend. That's why we called it *The Book of Outrageous Questions.* The questions included in this work are products of the author's imagination and fancy. No statement made about any person, product or place in any of these questions should be taken as true.

An *Original* Publication of POCKET BOOKS

 POCKET BOOKS, a division of Simon & Schuster Inc.
1230 Avenue of the Americas, New York, NY 10020

ISBN: 0-671-67299-1

First Pocket Books printing November 1988

10 9 8 7 6 5 4 3 2 1

POCKET and colophon are trademarks of
Simon & Schuster Inc.

Printed in the U.S.A.

Dedicated to:

Cindy, Russell, Rosemarie Grace and Joe, and especially to Mr. Horne with an "e," our 12th grade high school homeroom teacher.

Acknowledgments

Thanks to that great letter writer, Ben F., my other friends, Scott A., Sheila R., John C., Janet C., Tony G., Spaz, Lori, Baby Giuseppe, Millie, Irv, Sheri, Casey, Frank and Traie. Also thanks to Rhonda K. from the last time.

Contents

Introduction   11

Questions Not to Ask While in Confession   13

Questions to Ask While Waiting Behind
  a Fat Woman at a Self-help Cafeteria   21

Questions to Ask While on Line for the
  John   29

Questions Not to Ask Your Jail Cell
  Partner   41

Questions to Ask at a Bachelor Party   47

Questions Not to Ask Your New
  Supervisor   59

Questions to Ask While Waiting to Hear
  the Results of Your VD/AIDS Test   69

Questions Not to Ask Your Prospective
  In-laws   79

Questions to Ask While Awaiting
  Proctologist or Gyno Exam Results   89

Questions to Ask While Rearranging Your
  Sock Drawer   99

To be or not to be, that is the question . . .
                                                      —Shakespeare

And one hell of a question at that. What, my friends, did Willie actually mean by that? Did he really have an answer for his inquiry? Beats the shit out of me.

All through history great people have asked questions of others and of themselves. Through the ages great discoveries that have affected scores of people have been stumbled upon by people asking thought-provoking questions. Their brainstrains have gone on to shape life as we know it, and the future to come.

(If the truth be known, I wonder what earth-shattering discoveries have been made while sitting in the john.)

Fear not, my fun-loving and roguish readers, for this is not a book of questions to sweat and groan over. This is a book of outrageous, fun-filled questions that are a roar to ponder, a joy to mull, and a gas to chew the cud over!

11

We all have our dark sides, and this book will help you discover yours. It asks questions of you that no one else would have the guts to ask. There are no answers to these questions, only your innermost thoughts. Just don't answer with a simple yes or no. Be bold, dig deep where no one has probed before. These questions are here to help you reflect on all things you hold sacred and not so sacred.

Ask these questions of yourself, ask them of your lover. Don't ask them of your folks, no matter how young they are. Ask them of your friends and siblings. Don't ask them of your priest, rabbi, or minister. Ask them of your co-workers, but skip your boss or your personnel department.

So now, find out how low, how deviant, sexually perverse, racially prejudiced, uninhibited, immoral you are. Turn the page and be prepared to find out.

Questions Not to Ask
While in Confession

For ten thousand dollars, would you be willing to eat the individual ingredients in a hot dog?

Would you rather have a very large penis or have an overall great body?

If you had to kill your spouse, but did not have to worry about getting caught, how would you do it?

Would you go to the opera if all performances were nude, and they had farting contests during the intermissions?

If you could bring a weapon (but not a gun or exploding device), into the ring with you to fight Mike Tyson, what would it be? Why?

For ten thousand dollars, would you coldcock your grandmother? What if the only way to collect the money is if you knock her unconscious?

Are you loud in bed? Does this make you a better lover? Have you ever turned anyone off by being loud?

If you won ten million dollars in the lottery, what would you like to tell your present, over-bearing boss?

You are a heterosexual male attending a party. You are surrounded by beautiful women and equally handsome men. You have been flirting with some of the women and several of the apparently gay men have been giving you the eye. Suddenly, a major blackout puts the room in total darkness. Only seconds later, someone begins to caress your penis through your pants. What do you do?

For one million dollars, would you stick a glass rod up your ass and ride a motorcycle for a mile down a railroad track?

If you were a man, and you were marooned on a desert island with a young boy and no possible way of ever getting rescued, what female name would you wind up calling him?

If you were dressed like Shirley Temple and lying on the floor blowing the family dog when your in-laws walked in unexpectedly, what excuse would you use?

How would you describe two people fucking to a virgin blind man?

If you were on "The Newlywed Game" and the question was, "What does your wife's vagina smell like?", would you tell them the truth, or lose the game so as not to embarrass her?

For one million dollars, would you smear honey on your ass and sit on a bee hive for one hour?

How do double amputees masturbate?

If you were at work and, while taking a leak, got your penis painfully caught in your zipper and could not, no matter how hard you tried, get it out, whom would you call in to help you?

If your grandmother was dying and in great pain and she wanted you to put her out of her misery by killing her, but you had to use a sledgehammer, would you?

What is the largest thing the gay man with the largest asshole in the world would want to stick up his ass?

Have you ever left an obscene message on an answering machine? Was it a friend's or a stranger's?

Do you think a macho man is more comfortable in the presence of men or women?

How many famous Jewish male sex symbols can you name?

Sexually speaking, what is the difference between kinky and perverted?

How much money would you really need to live a life of total filth and debauchery?

Would you give up half of what you own for a pill that would allow you to bend your spine at will so you could blow/eat yourself?

Questions to Ask
While Waiting Behind
a Fat Woman at a
Self-help Cafeteria

When you were in elementary school, did the sound and sight of other kids throwing up start a chain reaction and make you sick, too?

How sexually experienced do you want your marriage partner to be? How much is too much?

Why are women with a lot of boyfriends considered sluts, but men with a lot of girlfriends considered studs?

If a feminist party developed, what would you suggest for their animal symbol?

How many slang words do you know for the penis? The vagina? Breasts? Anal sphincter?

Are men's penis sizes always in relation to the size of their hands?

If you are a woman, do bald heads turn you off? How about hairy bodies?

If you were in a restaurant with friends and they started to pick their noses, would you complain, or join in?

If you could have the last virgin in the world, would you deflower her?

How much physical pain would you be willing to endure to sleep with the sex symbol of your choice?

If the only way to get a fur coat was to skin the animals yourself, would you?

Whom would you love to see get fucked in the ass on national TV?

Which state do you think has the most stupid people? The most obnoxious? The most gays?

Do you kiss family members on the mouth? How about friends?

You are on a business trip with an associate of the same sex. He/she is less modest than you and walks around naked most of the time. Does it disturb you? Do you say anything?

To lower the child molestation rate, would you be in favor of using chastity belts?

How much money would it take to fill you with that "can't lose" confidence? If you had that amount, what awful things would you like to do and tell people who have pissed you off for years?

Would you like to have your mate's body featured in a porn magazine? Would it matter if it was a soft- or hard-core publication?

Would you eliminate a group of people to save your nation from financial ruin?

Which of the following makes your dick smaller?

A. Seeing your grandma naked
B. Taking a cold bath
C. Hearing about gerbils stuck up asses

Questions to Ask
While on Line
for the John

Do you like to read while on the toilet? What kind of reading material is your favorite?

You are a young high school teacher. The most attractive student in your twelfth grade homeroom is giving you the come-on. Would you risk your career for a one-night stand?

How much weight would you allow your mate to gain before you were turned off sexually?

What do you think of at the height of sexual climax?

Do you line the toilet seats in a public john? In a friend's house?

Do you lie about your sex life? In what way? Is it a little white lie, or an out-and-out fabrication?

Which drugs do you think enhance sex? Which ruin it?

When you can't perform sexually, do you blame yourself, or your partner?

Is sex worth the effort we put into getting it and doing it?

Which ethnic group, do you feel, has the most redeeming qualities? Which has the least?

Do Chinese driver's licenses have hair and eye color on them? If so, why?

If you were a male boss, would you hire a secretary for her body or for her skills? If you chose her for her body, would you make sure your office was always chilly?

Do you think they should put anatomically correct organs on Ken and Barbie dolls?

What nationality makes the best lover?

What do you feel constitutes a chronic masturbator? How often do you masturbate?

Have you ever peed in a public pool as an adult?

Have you ever gotten laid while there was someone else besides your lover in the room? Did it heighten the experience for you?

If you had lived in the late 1920s, would you have betrayed America to help Nazi Germany if you were certain they'd catch up with your landlord?

Would you date an attractive person even if you knew he or she did not shower after exercise class?

Would you sleep with your boss to get a better position at your company? What if you both were the same sex?

Should retarded people be allowed to get married and have children?

If you took a highly regarded aptitude test after you graduated from college, and it was interpreted as saying you were best suited to become an elevator operator, what would you do?

Are only the farts that are forced noisy?

Which ethnic group has the most body features that turn you on, and which has the most that turn you off?

If your daughter ever starred in a porno flick or caused a political scandal, would you disown her?

Do you believe that all black men have large dicks and that all Chinese men have small ones?

If you are a white man (woman) and had to marry a black woman (man), whom would you choose? And vice versa.

Does the sight of homosexuals making love revolt you or turn you on? Reverse this question if you are homosexual.

Would you stare unabashedly at an overly endowed person? Would it matter if the person was the same sex as you?

You are in a very important meeting with your new boss. He is charged up about your new assignment and starts to unwittingly spit out his words, right into your face. Do you say something, or do you endure it?

If you had pictures of your boss in a cross-dressing situation, would you blackmail him or her?

Which of the following is more legitimate?

A. Pro wrestling
B. TV preachers
C. A Howard Hughes will

Would you park a brand-new car in a Puerto Rican neighborhood at night?

If you were straight, and you were offered a great

job in a strictly homosexual workplace, would you take it?

Do you think you could be a good sex-education teacher? Explain your qualifications.

What would you rather do?

A. Spend five years on a deserted island with a beautiful girl/boy having nothing but sex
B. Spend five years in your favorite city having everything but sex

Which TV evangelist do you think is the most perverted?

If your adolescent daughter wears more makeup than you, has a bigger bust than you, and wears six-inch heels to school, are you to assume your "birds and bees talk" isn't necessary?

Would you shake someone's hand if you knew he never washed after using the john?

Questions Not to Ask
Your Jail Cell Partner

How would you feel if you were a handsome, blond, male heterosexual on your first night in jail?

Would you look down on someone whose genital size was far below normal? Would you bring it up in an argument?

Since we know good looks are fleeting, would you date a man with a nice personality, but more hair in his nose than on his head?

If you were at your boss's house for a dinner party and a dish being served was called Bung Hole Soup, would you just eat and not cause a scene, or would you satisfy your curiosity and ask what the hell it is?

If you come home from work and your wife has set up a complicated system of chains and pulleys in the bedroom, the mailman is wearing edible cock rings, and your wife looks like she's been snacking between meals, would a jury convict you?

Considering the shape of Japan's economy today, and their intelligence gain, was the nuking of Japan really a bad thing?

For how much of a raise would you really kiss your boss's ass in Macy's window?

Did somebody experiment with different types

of fruits and vegetables before settling on the phrase "cornhole"?

Would you, for one million dollars, dip your nuts into a pot of boiling water for one minute?

Which is worse?

A. Having your instructor die at ten thousand feet on your first private flying lesson
B. Getting your period in shark-infested water
C. Losing consciousness at a gerbil-laden gay party

If you could only perform one sexual act over and over for the rest of your life, or have an act performed on you over and over, what would you choose?

If you could change one thing about your spouse, physically, what would it be?

If medicine became so advanced that eyes, lungs, hearts, virtually all body parts could be replaced, would you live life more recklessly?

Do you get nervous around handicapped people? Would you ever date one?

If you and your best friend were in the woods, and he was bitten on the dick by a poisonous snake, and the only cure was to suck out the venom, would you?

Questions to Ask
at a Bachelor Party

If your son came home covered with dried sperm and with dead rodents trapped up his rectum, is it safe to assume that you will have to rely on your other children to give you grandchildren?

If you are a woman and you are forced to go down on another woman, but you can select who it will be, whom do you choose?

Is there really an Aunt Jemima or Uncle Ben? And is Farina their child?

How do scientists test tampons?

Who decided how long a rectal thermometer had to be?

Why is it that sometimes you can shit and wipe all day, and sometimes you can shit and wipe and there is nothing there?

Is it me, or is it fucking impossible to tell if someone is Chinese, Japanese, Korean, or Vietnamese?

Would you flaunt a lover of another race in front of friends and family?

What would you do if you caught a known Iranian terrorist unarmed? How many times?

Which is the sillier invention?

A. A wheel couch (instead of a wheel chair) for many people
B. Shoes with permanent socks inside
C. Toilet paper for dogs

If you are a male and you had to get fucked in the ass, whom would you choose to do it if you had the opportunity to make a selection?

Would you blow or eat yourself if you could? Would it affect your dating?

In this coming election, do you feel the team of Hitler and Mussolini would have a decent shot at winning?

If you were Gilligan, wouldn't you have killed the Skipper, Professor, and Mr. Howell, and fucked the shit out of the women?

In a boxing match, who wins, Moses or Jesus? Does God promote it or Don King?

Which would you rather have?

A. A wife who is a witch
B. A servant who is a Genie
C. An uncle who is a Martian
D. A mother who is a car

Does it bother you when people talk to you while you're on the bowl?

What do you think is worse?

A. An innocent man sent to prison
B. A woman being raped
C. A Jew having to buy retail

If you were a parent, which would be worse? If you found out your kid was:

A. Gay
B. A prostitute
C. A drug addict

Which ethnic group has gotten the worst deal?

A. Jews in Germany during World War II
B. Blacks in America during slavery
C. Catholics in Roman days

If man evolved from ape, is it possible for the process to reverse? If so, has it already started in Brooklyn?

Do you think car insurance rates should be determined by race, creed, color, sex, age, and any combination thereof?

If it became acceptable behavior to masturbate in public, would you consider it?

If a giant anus was chasing you in the desert, how would you defend yourself against it?

Do you think everyone has masturbated at least once? If someone says they haven't, are they lying?

If there was nothing wrong with dating and having sex with a person of any age, what is the youngest age you could see yourself with?

When an airplane goes down and the newspaper has a list of the dead passengers, do you scan the names to see if you knew anyone?

Questions Not to Ask
Your New Supervisor

If you could choose a garden vegetable shape as the new shape of your penis, what veggie would you choose? How about for women's tits?

Your grandmother tells you she feels faint and her medicine is hidden, for some strange reason, inside her panties and you must get it. Suddenly, she passes out. As you frantically pull her dress over her head to get into her panties, your entire family rushes into the room. What do you do?

If you could put all your sperm in a container for one year, how much, in liquid amounts, would you amass?

If the Germans won World War II, what is one major thing that immediately comes to mind that would be different today?

If prostitution were legalized, would you or not?

Who hits harder, Don Mattingly or Joel Steinberg?

Explain why a sculpture of a nude woman is considered art, but a photograph of a nude person is considered pornography?

Who do you think will die first?

A. Milton Berle
B. Bob Hope
C. George Burns

If you had to choose, would you rather enter a room with two pit bulls or a pond of piranha? What body part would go first?

What is more worthless?

A. The Queen of England
B. The United Nations
C. Any Democratic presidential candidate

If you found out that every ejaculation took one half-hour off your life, how would that affect the way you pleasure yourself, or make love?

When you watch a Jerry Lewis movie, do you think he is imitating one of "his kids"?

How do Eastern Indians have the dot put on their foreheads? Does it hurt to remove it?

Have you ever gotten a person drunk so you could take advantage of him or her? What beverage do you recommend?

How bad do you feel when you read about disaster in the Middle East when hanky heads, camel jockeys, and sand niggers get blown away?

Are all triathletes great jocks, or just fucking crazy?

Which is a sillier profession to pursue?

A. Anal masseuse
B. Pet chiropractor
C. Vaginal barber

Do you become shy when you're in a public john and someone sits down next to you in the adjoining booth? Do you listen to them, and do you feel they are listening to you?

What childhood episode involving your genitals do you remember most vividly?

If you had to choose someone to make love to your spouse, whom would you choose?

Which would you choose, if you could:

A. To age normally and get older and eventually die at the age of eighty; or
B. At the age of forty, you start moving back-

ward in age until you eventually become an infant, and then die a fetus after the same eighty years.

What pisses you off more?

A. When you are wiping your ass and the toilet paper is not strong enough and you wipe some shit on your hand
B. When you make a great meal, and in your haste to sit down, you drop it on the floor and it's all covered with dirt and hair
C. When you catch your dick in your zipper

Did you ever try the penis popcorn box stunt that was used in the movie "Diner," or something similar?

If you could change sexes for one day so you could be privy to one thing the other sex gets to do, would you change your sex and what would that one thing be?

If farting were considered a talent, how talented would you consider yourself?

If you lined up all your shit, firm stools only, end to end, would they reach the moon before you died?

If you had to be a blind black musician, whom would you choose?

Questions to Ask While Waiting to Hear the Results of Your VD/AIDS Test

If you had a gay relationship for one night, would you pitch, catch, or just eat?

If Jesse Jackson is elected president, does that mean the slogan that was famous many years ago will be changed to "A fried chicken in every pot and a Monte Carlo in every garage"?

Do you feel ugly people are attracted to each other? Should they be allowed to have children?

Would you ever consider marrying a rich old person of the opposite sex to get their money when they died?

Does your bowel movement effect your mood for the day? Are you in a better mood the more you shit?

If you are white, would you rather live in a beautiful, opulent house in a black neighborhood, or live in a plain, average house in an all-white neighborhood? Reverse the situation if you are black.

If you had to grow hair on a part of your body where you normally don't have hair, where would you choose and why?

Do you feel that small-breasted women are smarter than large-breasted women?

Do you remember the first time you jerked off? Was it with friends or alone? Do you remember what you thought about? Did you have any idea what to expect?

Do women who have stronger vaginal muscles also have a stronger say in a relationship?

Do you become more aggressive than normal behind the wheel of a car? Do you cut off old ladies, Orientals, and assholes with "Baby on Board" signs?

What would you do or say if someone pissed on your legs while you were standing at a urinal?

Do you curl your toes or stretch them out during an orgasm?

73

For one million bucks, would you stick your head up an elephant's ass after it had diarrhea?

Would you lick off Tammy Faye Bakker's make-up for ten thousand dollars?

For one million dollars, would you masturbate with Ben Gay for one month?

How do you feel about the expression concerning breasts, "anything bigger than a mouthful is a waste"?

You are a white person who needs a transplant. During surgery, you are given a black person's heart. Would you consider it a coincidence if you began craving fried chicken and watermelon?

If the U.S. had a female president, would she have to be kept away from "The Button" once a month? Would PMS be a legitimate reason to take a week off every month?

If you had to drink one of the following to save your mother's life, which would you choose?

A. A cup of sperm
B. A cup of urine
C. A cup of diarrhea

Would it make a difference if you could pick a person to be the provider?

If you had to, which would you choose?

A. Lick a gay's toilet seat
B. Eat out a fat, black, old woman
C. Stick your nose in a dog's ass for five minutes

If you enjoy smelling your own farts, does that mean you would eat your own shit?

If you pass gas in the company of others in your own home, do you blame the family dog?

If you had to, which would you wear on your face for a week?

A. A baby's used diaper
B. Wilt Chamberlain's used jock
C. Oprah Winfrey's used panties

During the process of evolution, do you get a choice whether to continue on or stop where you are?

From where do you think the expression "blow" in relationship to oral sex came?

Which would you like to see most?

A. Someone lick his or her own genitals
B. Someone rip off somebody's head and shit down his neck
C. Gays inserting gerbils up their asses

If inanimate objects had feelings, what would you feel the most sorry for?

A. A handkerchief
B. A tampon
C. Toilet paper

Questions Not to Ask
Your Prospective In-laws

If you had a strong suspicion that the person you were in love with was a mass murderer, would you continue your relationship as long as it was never proved?

If you had to have either a three-inch penis, or a two-foot penis, which would you choose? How would it affect your sex life?

If you were a thirty-five-year-old woman stranded on a desert island with your seventeen-year-old son for five years with no hope of being saved, would you have sex with him? If you were the boy, would you forcibly rape your mother after five years without sex? How would you react if you were the father in this situation with your daughter?

If you were a smoker, and you found out that if you gave up smoking, you would live to be ninety, but if you continued to smoke, you'd live to be eighty-five, would you continue?

How do you think your penis, or your lover's penis, stacks up when compared with those of other men in the populace? In what percentile?

Do you think that, because women are getting more dominant and aggressive, the next step in the evolutionary chain is a vagina with teeth?

If you were making love, and during passionate romping, as you ran your fingers through his/her hair, you pull his/her wig off and find he's/she's as bald as a baby's behind underneath, what would you say or do next?

When women lose weight, their tits get smaller. Why don't dicks get smaller when men lose weight? Also, if a dick is muscle, how come it doesn't get flabby or atrophied like an arm or a leg?

Would you eat food off the floor? Of all the people you know, whose floor wouldn't you eat off of?

If you were walking through a gay part of town and came across an obvious homosexual in need of mouth-to-mouth resuscitation, would you help out?

Do you think the Pope jerks off? Does he fantasize about naked monks?

Has anyone ever really seen balls turn blue?

If men had testicles the size of bowling balls and women had tits the size of watermelons, what sports would be most affected?

Have you ever heard or witnessed your parents making love?

What was the most sexually bizarre act you have ever performed on another person?

If it was medically accepted and approved, would you use a product such as a reusable douche or condom if it could save you thousands of dollars over a lifetime?

If you are a heterosexual (homosexual), have you ever fantasized about someone of the same (different) sex?

Do fat people in tight clothes gross you out?

What do you think is fair punishment for a person who commits rape? Would having his balls pounded into veal patties suffice?

Would you date a hermaphrodite (half man/half woman)?

Have you ever faked an orgasm (if you are a woman)? Can men fake orgasms?

Does sexy underwear turn you on? What colors in particular?

Would you pierce your nipples for five thousand dollars?

What do foot fetishes stem from?

When you see a black male behind the wheel of an expensive car, do you always think he's either a pimp, a drug dealer, or a car thief?

What part of the body turns you on the most?

The elephant is the symbol for the Republican party and the donkey is the symbol for the Democratic party. If Jesse Jackson were an independent, would a chimp be the symbol of his party?

If abortions become illegal, should anti-abortionists be made to adopt one child every five years to help keep orphanages from becoming overcrowded?

Do you think people with certain exciting occupations (dangerous, athletic, etc.) make better lovers?

Could you make love to a quadriplegic? How many drinks would it take?

You and your spouse are constantly fighting over his/her weight. A new pill is discovered that is guaranteed to make the consumer lose weight. Would you hide it in your spouse's food every night?

How many vaginal crabs would constitute a seafood dinner? More than one pussy? (And is the plural of pussy "pussi"?)

Which of the following is the funniest joke book ever written?

A. *Outrageously Offensive Jokes*
B. *Outrageously Offensive Jokes II*
C. *Outrageously Offensive Jokes III*
D. *Outrageously Offensive Jokes IV*

If you are white, how much money would it take to get you into a Harlem movie theater to view *Crush Groove*?

Questions to Ask While Awaiting Proctologist or Gyno Exam Results

If you were pregnant and, after a sonogram, you were told that the fetus was terribly deformed, would you have an abortion, or name the child "Baby Geek" and make money by selling it to a sideshow?

If you put a person on the guillotine and chop his head off in a split second, how much time would go by before the person is dead, or does the person actually think for a few seconds while his head is detached from the body?

You and your spouse, with whom you're deeply in love, are killed together in a car accident. At the Pearly Gates, St. Peter proclaims that your spouse is going to hell, and you have the choice of joining him/her, or going to heaven. What would you choose?

If you found out that your wife took all your money, was fucking your best friend, and drove your children to hate you, how many times would you hit her with a sledgehammer?

How many women do you personally know who like to perform fellatio?

Would you like it if, every time a man got an erection, or a woman got hot, their nose lit up bright red for all to see? Would it help in singles bars?

What is your favorite part of your spouse's/lover's anatomy?

You are in the shower, you slip and fall, and the soap goes up your ass. If your lover comes in and asks to borrow the soap, do you explain the truth, or make up some story?

If you were in a bar and a person of the opposite sex tried to pick you up, do you have any limitations on age? What's your cut-off limit?

If you woke up in the middle of the woods with your pants down to your knees and your asshole sore and red, would you tell anyone?

Do you like to make love to the sound of music? Do you stroke to the beat?

What is your favorite sexual activity? Does it enhance sex for your partner?

If you could be reborn, would you come back as a porn star, an athlete destined to become a drug addict, or a millionaire without any legs?

Does watching animals having sex turn you on?

How will evolution affect our sex organs three hundred years from now?

Which positions do you think Jimmy Swaggart asked the hooker to perform so he could watch and whack his pepperoni?

Who has the nastiest reputation?

A. Ayatollah Khomeini
B. Muhammar Qaddafi
C. Yassir Arafat
D. Ferdinand Marcos
E. Morton Downey, Jr.

You can use a voodoo doll to hurt someone, but can you also use a voodoo doll to pleasure someone? If you stick a pin in a doll's stomach, the person it represents gets a sharp stomach pain, but if you were to lick the doll's groin area, would the person it represents get turned on?

If a father never knew his daughter, and years later, picked her up in a bar and boffed her, is that considered incest?

Must you be a bilingual waitress to serve people in an International House of Pancakes?

What would you consider worse?

A. Shooting a bowling ball into a pregnant lady's stomach
B. Hitting a man's penis, which is lying on an anvil, with a sledgehammer
C. Putting plastic explosives on a woman's nipples, then detonating them

What personal habit do you find most offensive: farting, belching, or nose-picking?

What would you rather do: pick someone's nose or wipe someone's ass?

Your lover wants to experiment with sex toys. He promises that they will enrich your sex life. He admits that some may cause discomfort while getting used to them, but that he would never cause you any real pain. Do you go along with him?

Do overweight people eating fattening foods drive you wild?

If people crapped out of their mouths and ate with their asses, would it make rich people humble and liven up boring dinner parties?

Would you continue smoking your brand of cigarettes if they increased the amount of saltpeter in them?

If you could make pussy taste like anything other than fish, what would it be?

At a party, which would be more embarrassing?

A. Having an oozing pimple on your nose the size of a golf ball
B. Losing control of your bowels in the middle of a dance

C. Having too much to drink and vomiting on
   your hostess

If you could have X-ray vision, which one of
your other senses would you be willing to give
up?

Questions to Ask While Rearranging Your Sock Drawer

Have you ever padded your clothing to give the impression that you were better endowed than you really are?

If money grew on trees, would more Jews become farmers rather than doctors?

Does an eye doctor in China get half pay? Does he bother to say, "Open wide"?

If you were in the delivery room waiting for your first child, and the baby came out a different color than you and your wife, what would you do?

Do you like the smell of your own farts?

Do you feel that the expression "it's not how much you have, it's how you use it" is true?

Do you like to squeeze other peoples' pimples and blackheads?

If you are a heterosexual and were stranded in the desert and the first place you came to was a gay bar, would you enter?

Have you ever exposed yourself to a small child, even unwittingly?

Have you ever lost control of your bowels or bladder as an adult?

If Charles Manson, Ted Bundy, and David "Son of Sam" Berkowitz are all in the same room with you, who are you least afraid of? Most afraid of?

Do you feel that anyone who uses a dating service is automatically a loser?

The ad in the paper says, "Hung like a bull. This thirty-year-old S/W/J/M/ momma's boy uses his pecker for a bat. Looking for blond, leggy beauty. Must have huge tits. No dogs. Photos a must." Do you answer?

Do you ever feel glad when you see a very expensive car broken down on the side of the road?

If farts became a viable fuel alternative, would big fat slobs be looked at in a more positive light?

Would you go down on a gorgeous member of the opposite sex if it smelled like a limberger cheese party the closer you got to home base?

Do you think people in prison should be used for experiments in lieu of animals? The more hideous the crime, the more bizarre the experiments?

There is only one other person in the room with you and you silently fart. How do you handle it?

Would you mention to someone that he had snot hanging from his nose? Would it matter if you knew the person or not?

If all blacks disappeared, would the quality of professional sports decline?

What race do you think is the missing link between ape and man?

Does the fact that all women's vaginas smell like fish prove that all life started in the ocean?

What one movie scene do you recall that turned you on so much that you couldn't wait to go home and act it out with either a lover or by yourself?

If you lived in a house, and one night evil, weird voices said, "Get out," what would you do?

A group of female aliens landed on earth. They were as pretty as Playboy bunnies, but they had large male genitals. If you were an Earthling male, would you be considered gay if you fucked them?

Have you ever fantasized about a family member? If you knew that you would never be discovered, would you ever act out your fantasy?

What is the most amount of weight one person can lose while shitting during one sit-down session?

If you and your friends had to shit in a separate pile for a year, who would compile the largest turd mountain?

If you were bald and you had to wear one of the following, which would you choose?

A. A vagina
B. An underarm
C. A floppy dog ear

Do you think masturbation increases or decreases IQ?

Do you feel condoms in different ethnic skin tones have social value?

If you were forced to have sex with an animal, what kind would you choose?

What percentage of priests, do you think, whack their carrots? What percentage of nuns plump their puddin'?

If the AMA came out and said, after extensive testing, that shit is the most nutritious thing you could eat, it has no calories, and companies could flavor it to any taste, would you eat it?

Using physical features from famous people, living and/or dead, what would your most sexy and desirable lover look like?

If an Iranian's head was on fire, and there was no water available, would you piss on it?

What would you say is the best substitute for a vagina?

A. A toupee with a can of tuna dumped on it
B. A fish with artificial hair plugs
C. A rotting Jello mold with Brillo pads in it

Describe, in sexual terms, the perfect marriage. How much sex? What type of sex? Is there always a dominant person?

Should condoms be given out in prison and should French ticklers be available on request?

If you're a pilot and you fly past the speed of sound, can you hear your own fart?

Why do people in cars feel compelled to pick their noses while stuck in traffic?

What childhood trauma would have persuaded someone to become a proctologist or a stool analyzer?

If an obviously gay man comes into your pet store and wants to buy a gerbil, do you sell it to him?

For one million dollars, would you play tackle football with a light bulb in your underwear?

List animals, other than gerbils, that gays could realistically use as a sexual aid.